MY REFLECTION

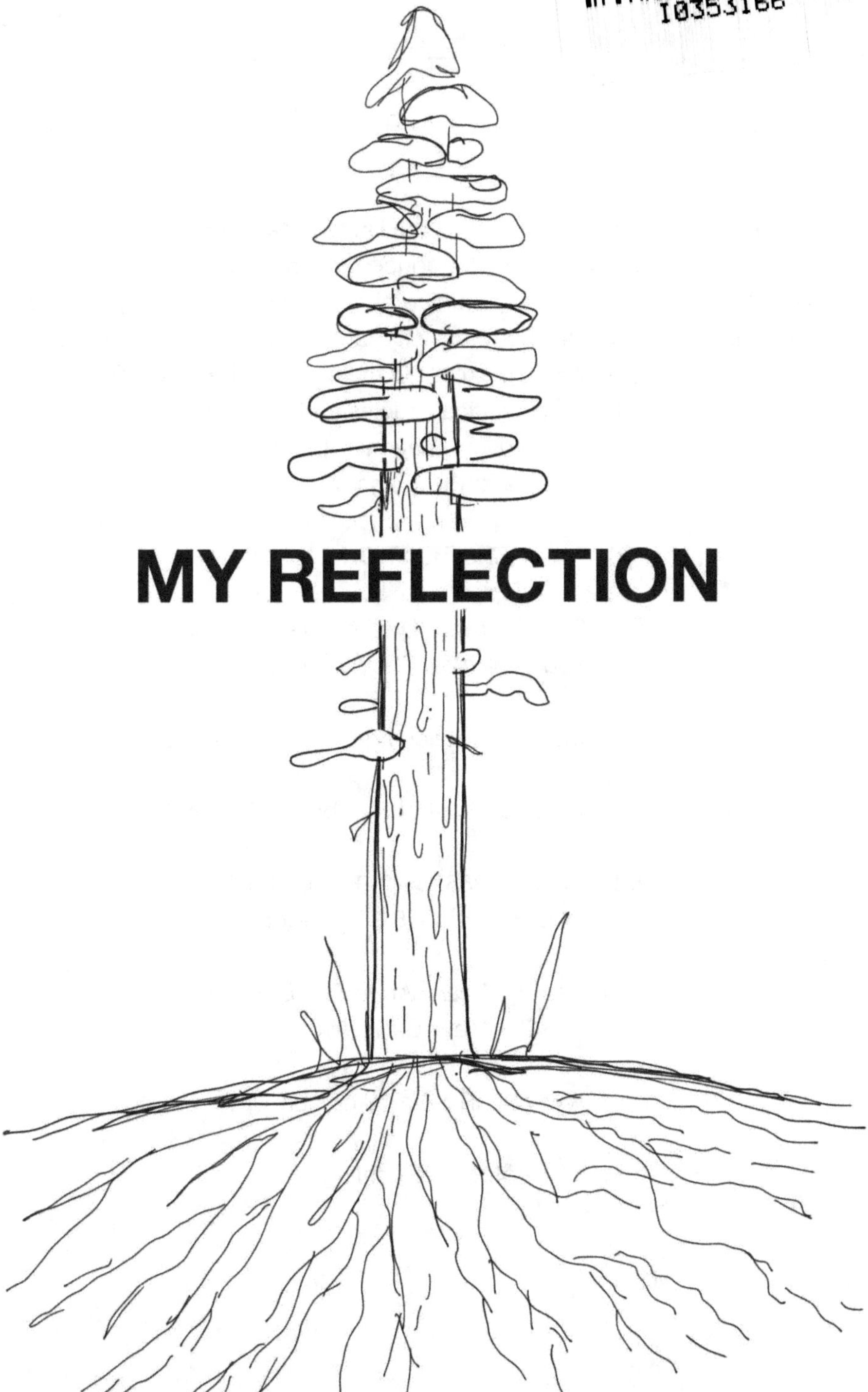

Copyright © 2021 by Neal Eisler

All rights reserved. Printed in the United States of America.
No part of this book may be reproduced, distributed, or transmitted in any form or by any means, including photocopying, recording, or other electronic or mechanical methods, without the prior written permission of the author, Neal Eisler, except in the case of brief quotations embodied in critical articles and reviews.
For more information, address:
NealTheEarthling@gmail.com.

FIRST EDITION

Illustrations by Lyn The Alien
Poetry by Neal The Earthling

Library of Congress Cataloging-in-Publication Data

Library of Congress Control Number: 2021939313

ISBN 978-1-7353554-2-9 (paperback)
ISBN 978-1-7353554-3-6 (eBook)

Published by *Dream World Publishing*™
Oak View, California

www.NealTheEarthling.com

@NealTheEarthling

Thank you to all HUMANS BEING,

For guiding me to detect the undetected...

Helping me see my reflection;
Helping me stop my insurrection;
Helping me start my introspection.

For watching me grow,
Teaching me all that I know.

For sharing and for caring,
Understanding and opening me up.

For bringing out the best of me,
Helping me rid myself of the worst.

For guiding me to find beauty in reality,
Showing me infinite capability.

Security in this knowledge
Has erased insecurity I can now acknowledge.

An insistence on resistance; ignorance,
A constant persistence.

Unseeing vision misleading.

Days speeding bye,
Egos bleeding tie.

For, thanks to you,
I no longer have to wonder why.

                    -Neal

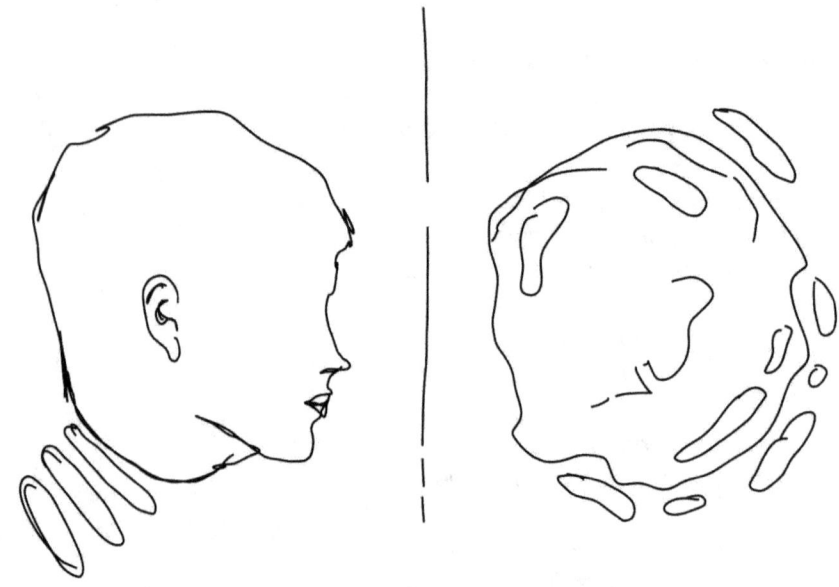

*Dedicated to those of you,
Who struggle to see
Your true reflection.*

MY REFLECTION

Written by Neal The Earthling
Illustrated by Lyn The Alien

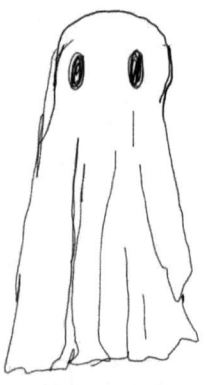

MY GHOST
PROLOGUE

A GHOST,
Hidden in plain sight.

UNABLE TO SEE ANY LIGHT,
Only the dark night.

ITS REFLECTION WASN'T BRIGHT.

A CREATURE,
Who wants to step out.

One trying to go about,
BURIED BENEATH LOUD SHOUTS!

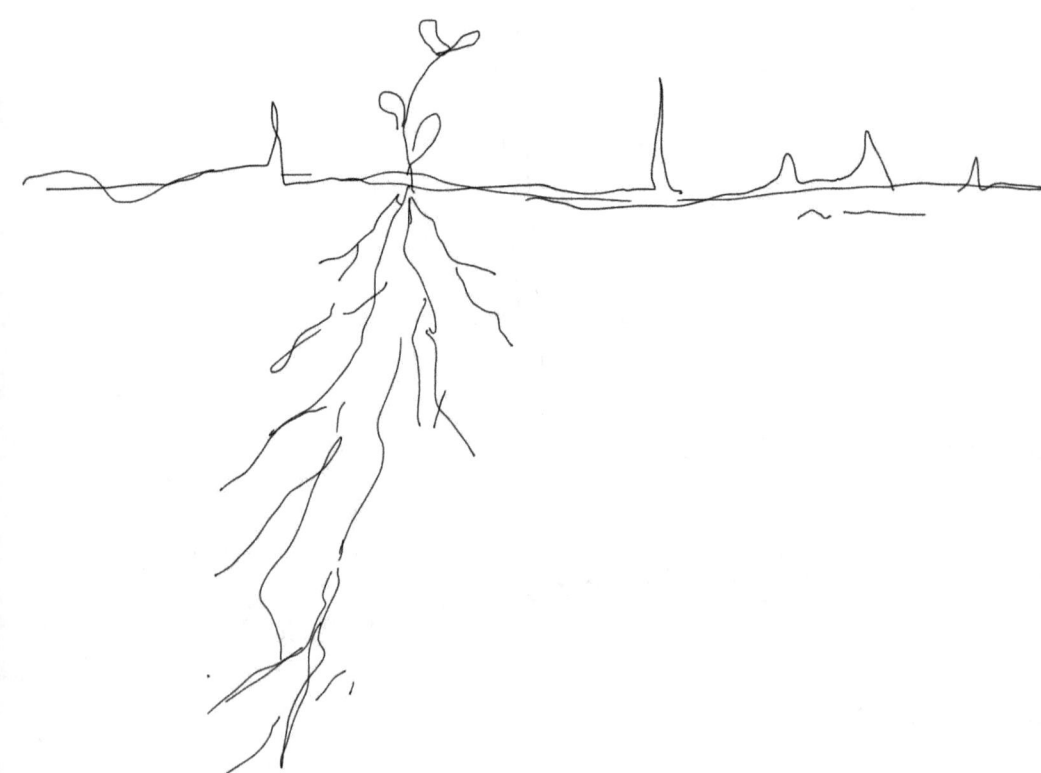

A QUESTION
As to identity...

WHERE DOES ONE FIT IN?

Can that be all, Start to crawl,
Before we fall? To be so tall?

Under a cloak,
Truth bespoke.

This ghost awoke,
Poke after poke.

Until it burned,
Life turned.

Relationships mourned,
Death transformed.

A GHOST,
Hidden in plain sight.

UNABLE TO SEE ANY LIGHT,
Only the dark night.

Killing off our actor,
No longer a factor.

Taking life from the hands of others
Placing it back in our own...

A CHILDISH MOAN NO LONGER SHOWN.

From the inside out,   From the inside out.
This ghost comes about. This ghost comes about.

Hidden no longer,
Feeling stronger.

Taking on meaning,
Shining and beaming.

Brighter than bright,
        TRUTH
            WON
                THIS
                    FIGHT.

Goodbye ghosts of my past,
I'm here at last.

I'M HERE AT LAST,
HERE, AT LAST.

   AT LAST   AT LAST   AT LAST

UNTIL

I'M

CAUGHT

BACK

IN THE PAST.

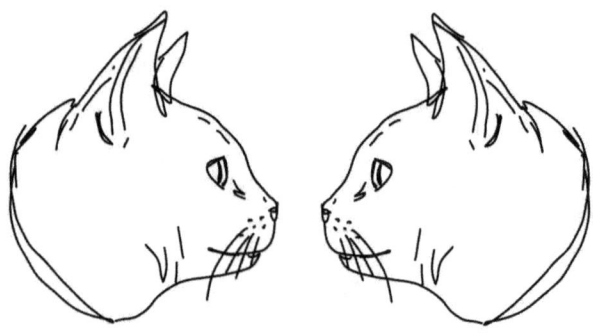

COPYCAT

You are copying me
You lie to me.

You can't see me
You can't be me.

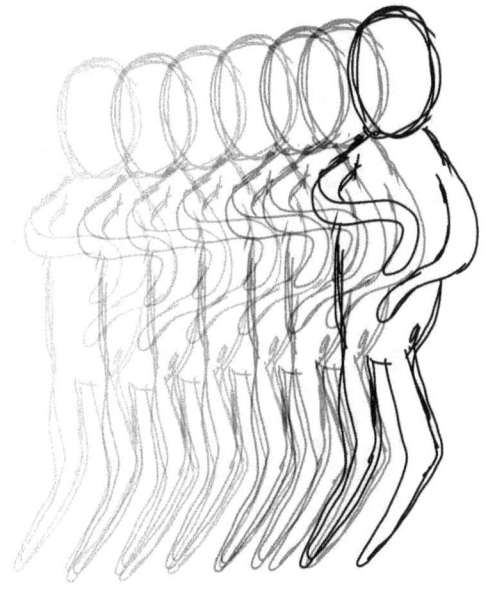

Don't copy me...

**DON'T
    COPY
        ME!**
DON'T
    COPY
        ME!

Copycat
LIKE A RAT.

A rat a tat tat
Some chit chat.

Going to bat...

COPY,
    COPY,
COPY,   **COPYCAT!**
    COPY,
        COPYCAT!

Falling flat
There you sat.

Little brat
YOU COPYCAT.

Don't copy me...

**DON'T
COPY
ME!**

'CAN'T YOU SEE?'

Can't you see,
You are copying me.

I'm the first
With this thirst...

TIME TO BURST.

You are...

**YOU ARE
 THE WORST!**

An originator
You came later; traitor,
FALL INTO A CRATER!

Don't copy me,
DON'T
COPY
ME!

CAN'T YOU SEE?
CAN'T YOU SEE?

Can't you see,
You are copying me.

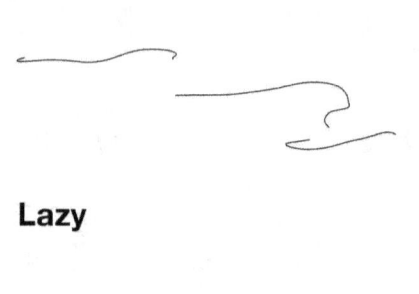

Lazy

Crazy,

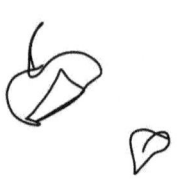

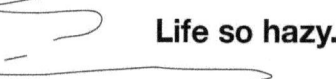

Life so hazy.

Rank

Blank,

To be frank.

You copy me
You copy me.

You copy me,
CAN'T YOU SEE?

Can't you see,
YOU COPY ME.

You copy me
You copy me.

**YOU COPY ME
YOU COPY ME!**

Alien to me,
Why can't you see?

WHY CAN'T YOU BE?
WHY CAN'T YOU BE?

Why can't you be
          FREE,
                FREE,
                      FREE?

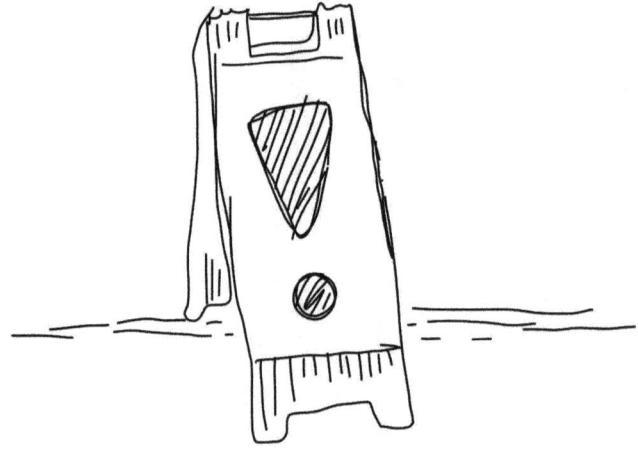

ATTENTION

Attention,
ATTENTION!

Give me some
I'm not done,
I'M THE ONLY ONE.

I'M THE ONLY ONE.

I'M THE ONLY ONE.

I'M THE ONLY ONE.

I'M THE ONLY ONE.

I'M THE ONLY ONE.

I'M THE ONLY ONE.

Give me attention,
PAY ATTENTION.

Give me a sign,
TELL ME IT'S FINE.

I don't want to whine,
I JUST WANT TO SHINE.

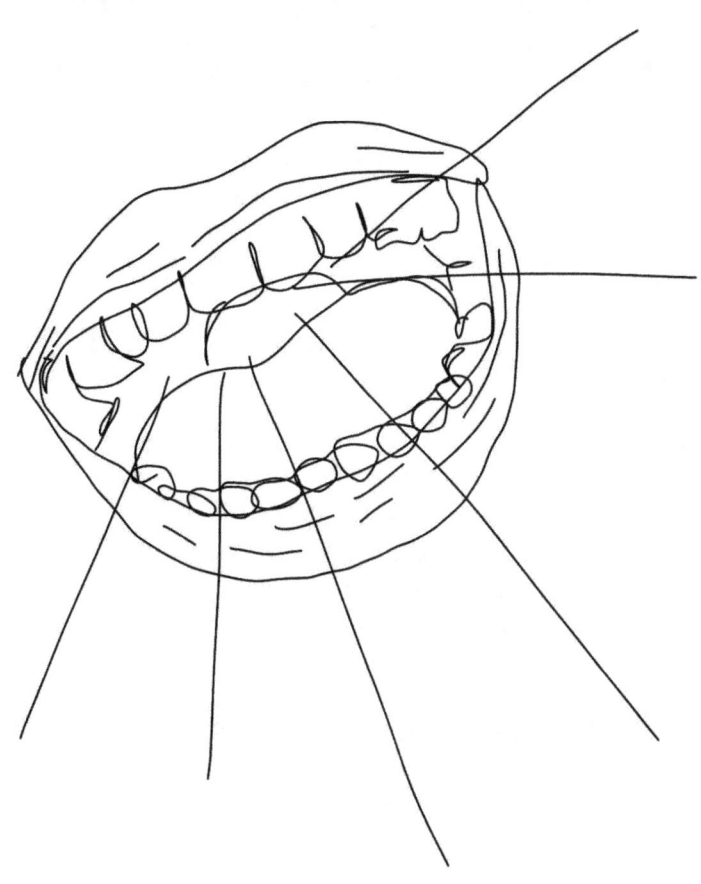

ATTENTION!

        Over there
        LOOK HERE,
        SO NEAR
        To seeing clear.

I want attention
Not reprehension.

What I would pay
For something to say.

      Attention...
      Is all I want,
      Attention...

              Pay me some
              Or, I'll feel shunned.

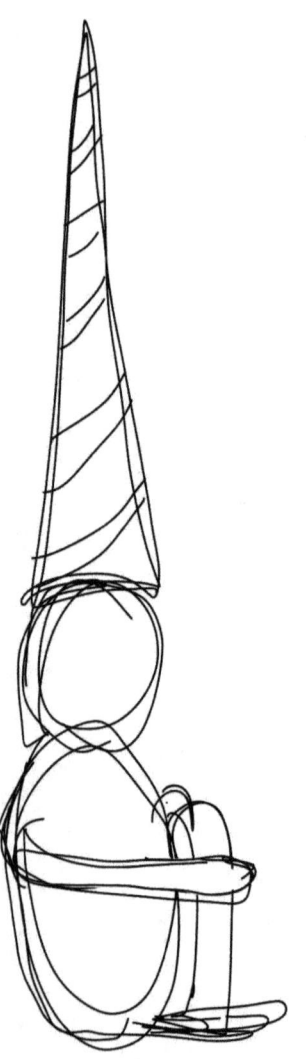

Addicted, conflicted,
My mind is constricted.

Feeling inadequate
Lacking adequacy,

        Attention,
        ATTENTION,
        Please help me see.

                Unable to see
                MY ATTENTION IS ME.

                UNABLE TO SEE
                My attention is me.

                My attentive plea,
                PLEASE SET ME FREE.
                PLEASE SET ME FREE.
                PLEASE SET ME FREE.

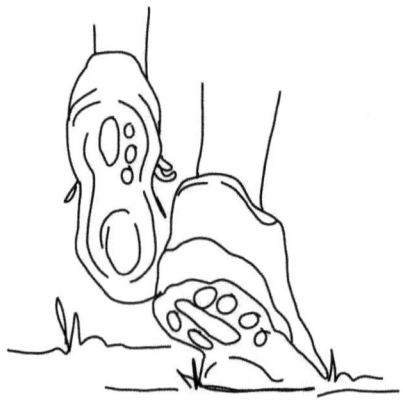

RUNNING

The more attention you seek,
The less happy you become.

Running
On the run,
Your mind is spun.

**STOP RUNNING
STOP HIDING,**
From those who are chiding.

Face those
Who have done you wrong
                      Head on,
                      BE STRONG.

USE YOUR VOICE,
It's your choice.

      SPEAK TRUTH TO POWER,
      Don't ever cower.

           **STAND TALL
           LIKE A TOWER,**
           Looking down
           From atop the wall.

           **BEFORE YOU FALL
           PLEASE HEAR YOUR CALL.**
                  PLEASE HEAR YOUR CALL.
                  PLEASE HEAR YOUR CALL.

Aggression leads to possession,
Your mind becomes obsession.

OWNED.

Remember passivity
Leads to relativity,
GROUNDED IN REALITY.

Spreading compassion
For all to see,
NOT CAVING TO BRUTATLITY.

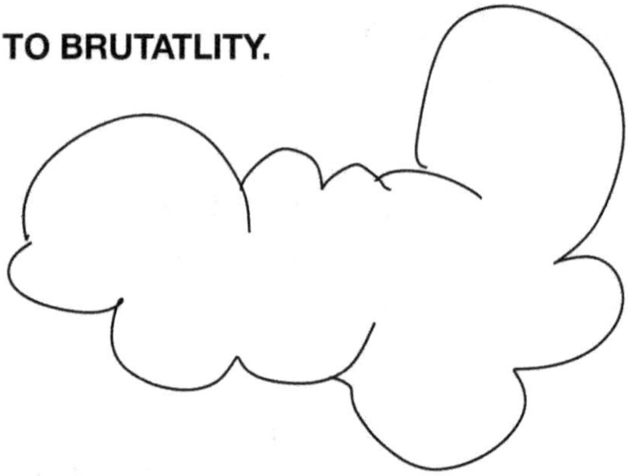

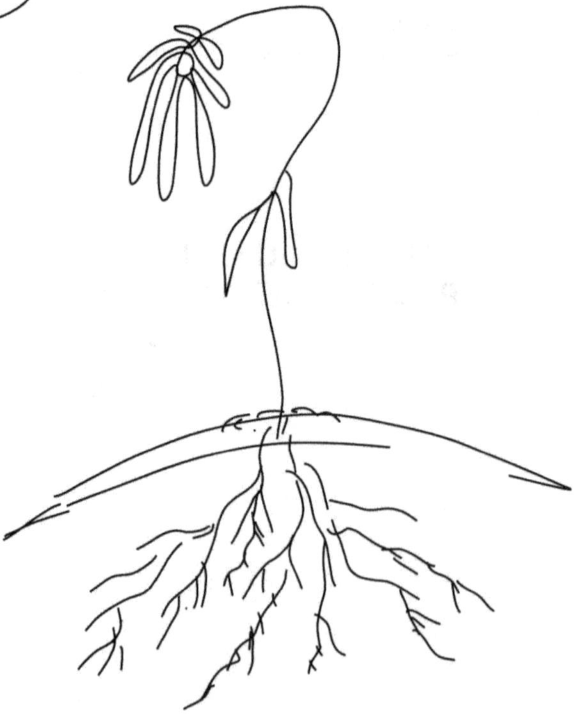

Standing up to your bully
Their abusing ways,
See beyond haze
Each neglectful gaze.

Physical violence
A verbal alliance.

Viral attacks
Taunting tacts.

WHAT COUNTERACTS HOW THEY ACT?
WHAT COUNTERACTS HOW THEY ACT?

**NON-VIOLENCE
A PEACE ALLIANCE.**

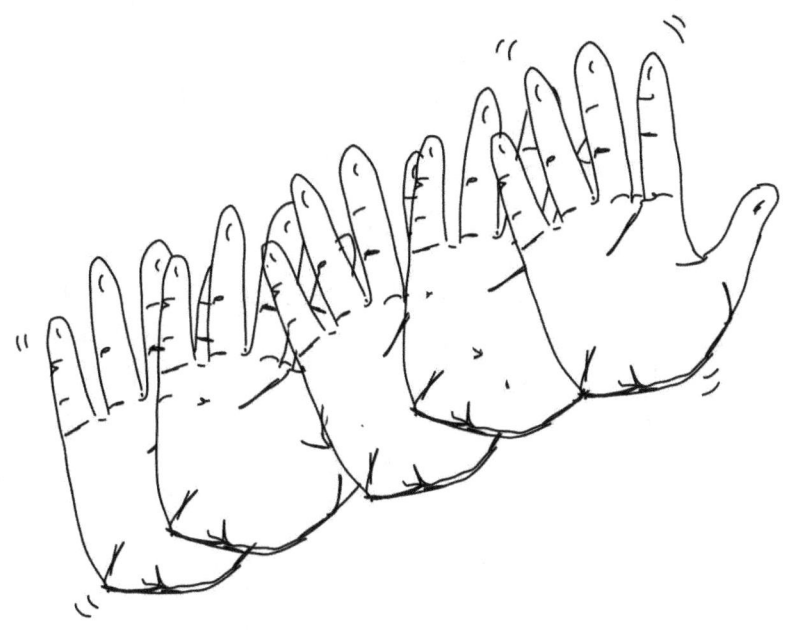

Stand up to your bully
Their abusing way,
End each play
With a peaceful array.

Turning a blind eye
Not letting them see you cry,
IGNORING EACH LIE
    AFTER LIE,
        AFTER LIE...

        Kissing them goodbye.

            GOODBYE.

WHOSE THE REAL LOSER?
Let's call it the abuser.

They struggle too
But misconstrue,
Trying to control you
So you can feel too.

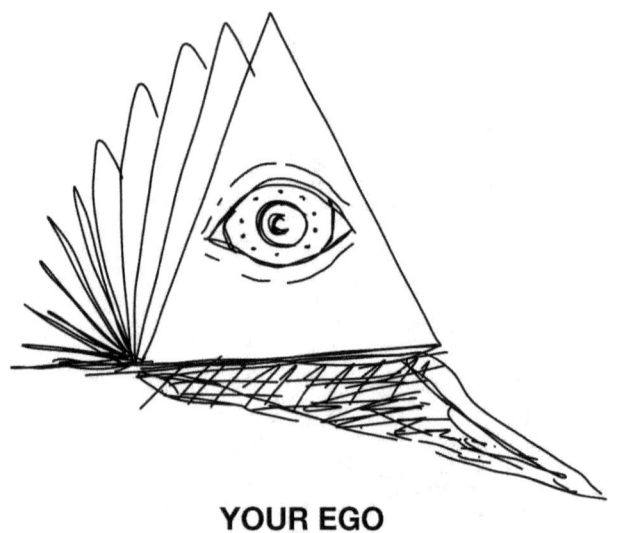

YOUR EGO

Sometimes people's ego
Shines brighter than
The light inside of them.

Confused, bruised...

Raging out of control,
Influenced by intoxication.

NO RELATION TO ONESELF.

But **DELUSIONS**
That become **CONCLUSIONS.**

Projection of misery

Everything getting dizzy.

      Building anger
      Creating danger.

           Danger,
                    Danger,
                            Danger!

Trying to make
Everyone feel the same
While you go insane,
No one else to blame.

Feel shame. **FEEL SHAME.**

Shame, shame,
SHAME ON YOU.

We are not playing this game,
Not anymore...

**WE HAVE ALL THE TIME
IN THE WORLD.**

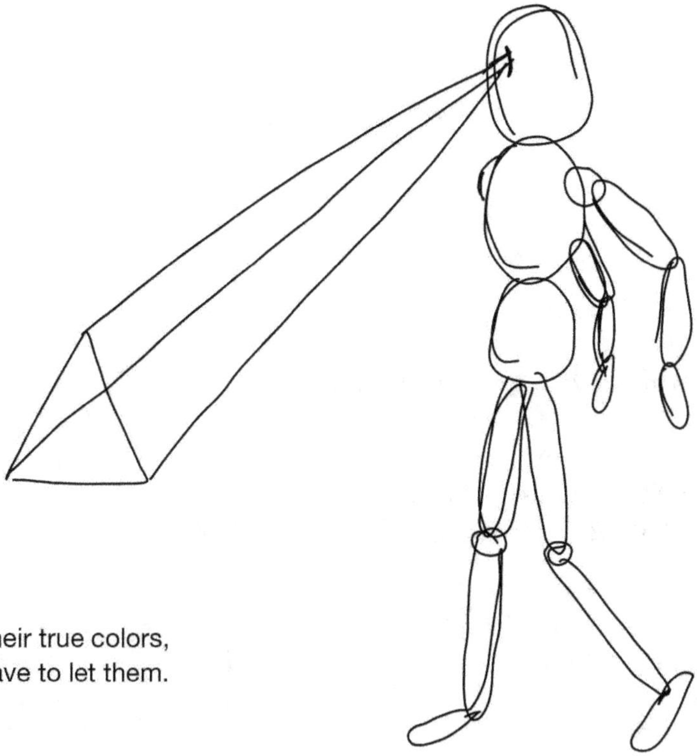

People show their true colors,
And you just have to let them.

Sometimes it's projection,
Of things
They are letting affect them.

Soon it becomes infection.

Don't let your ego shine bright.

**STOP YOUR FIGHT
FIND BEAUTIFUL LIGHT.**

Unfortunately, you can't...

And, your ego shines brighter
Than the light inside of you.

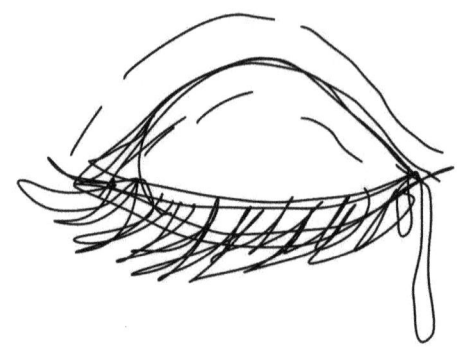

MY BULLY BRO

Don't copy me
Can't you see?

YOU ARE THE WORST!

Push,
   Shove...
         Attack,
              Smack!

A bully who knows me
A bully he sees me,
A bully scares me so.

This bully bro
Puts out my glow,
Which makes it hard to grow.

Oh no, oh no...

                No,

                          No!

                                  No

                                No

                                     No

                                       No

                                           No.

Fear,
　　　　Smear...
　　　　　　　　　Lie,
　　　　　　　　　　　　Hide!

Afraid to show
This bully bro,
My honest human glow.

A bully who knows me
A bully he sees me,
A bully scares me so.

Find
Kind,
Remind
Don't be blind.

Don't be blind,
Remind, **REMIND.**

Be Kind,
In that, **YOU'LL FIND.**

LOVE
A dove.

PEACE
A smile grease.

Bully bro you've got to go...

You don't know,
You don't know me so,

Bully bro you've got to go.

      Go,

          Go,

              GO!

No, no!
Say's bully bro.

This is my show!

You are...
You are in my show, bro!

Don't let up
GET UP,
Step up
STAND UP.

        Bully bro you've got to go,
            You've got to go
           YOU'VE GOT TO GO!

                    Go,

                            Go,

                                  GO!

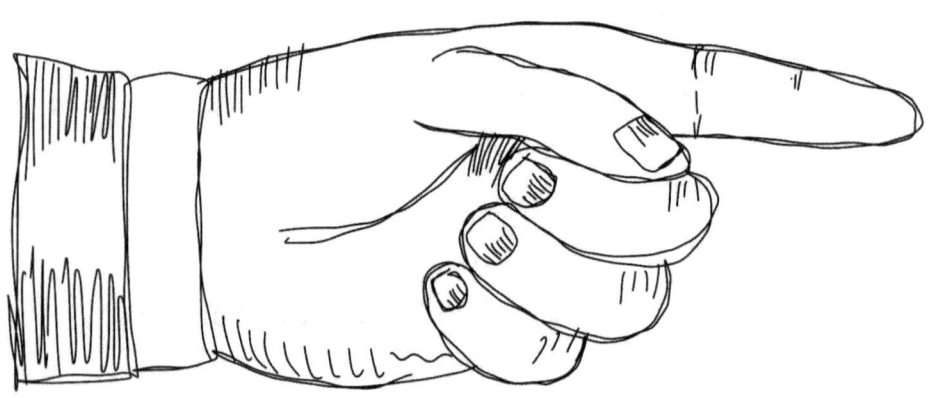

You've got to go
My bully bro,
This is no longer your show.

This is my show.

'THIS IS MY SHOW!'

                                                      This is my show,
                                                     I'll let you know.

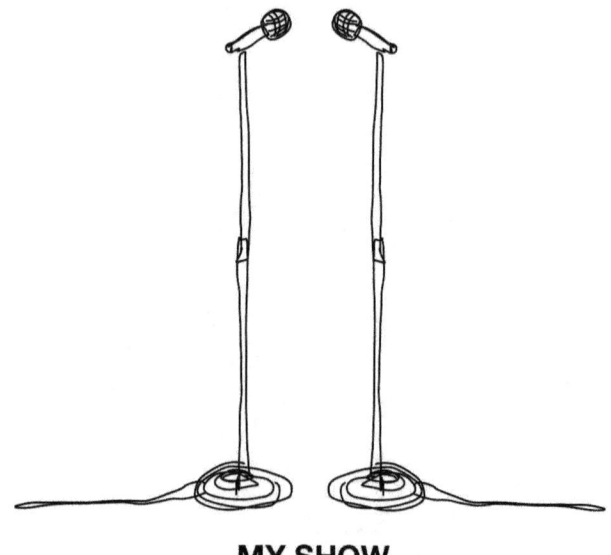

MY SHOW
MY GLOW,
MY FLOW

Just so you know.

Just so you know
Just so you know,

THIS IS MY SHOW.

I'll make it slow
I'll find my flow,
Outside each blow.

You punched me bro,
    I said no,
                No,
        no   **NO!**
               No,
                    NO!

        YOU COULDN'T GROW
        NOW YOU KNOW.

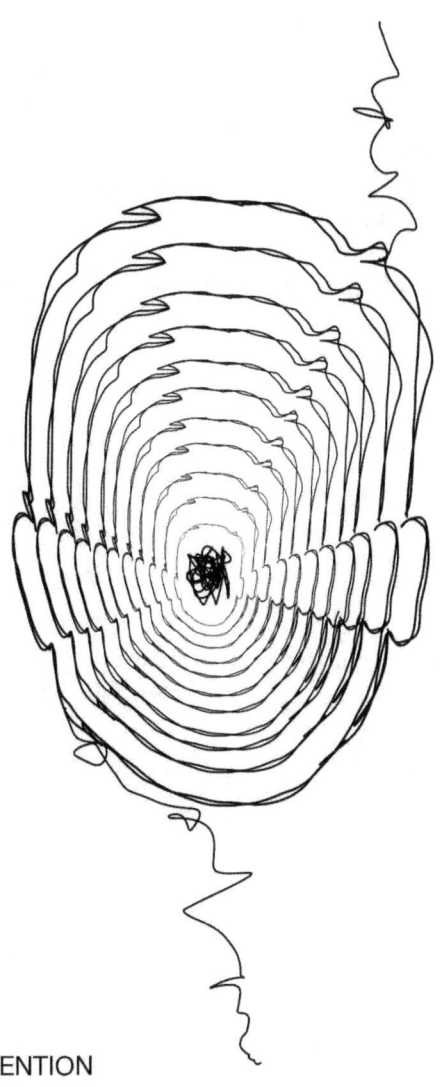

Hurt inside,
You tried, you tried.

        TO DRAW ATTENTION
        With aggressive intention.

                There's no exception
                VIOLENCE IS REPRESSION.

Controlling
Patrolling,
Haunting dreams

SCARING SCREAMS.

          Stop!

      STOP!   **'STOP!'**

                         'STOP!'

**Ending in despair
TRAUMA TO REPAIR.**

But, I no longer fear
I still do care.

Forgive your act
Choose to counteract.

With compassion once lacked,
That is a fact.

THROUGH THE LOOKING GLASS

This looking glass through which I see,
A paradigm, my mind not truly free.

Please oh please
Can't you see,
This life is not
How it's supposed to be.

Stuck in place
Out of space,
No grace
Two-faced.

This looking glass through which I see,
A paradigm, my mind not truly free.

Released from the bind
Of the bullying kind,
Putting what's past behind
In my presence, you will find.

This looking glass no longer me,
My mind set free
Allowing me to be...

Truly, truly, truly free,
Truly free for all to see.

See a mind that's truly free,
THIS LOOKING GLASS NO LONGER ME.

MY REFLECTION

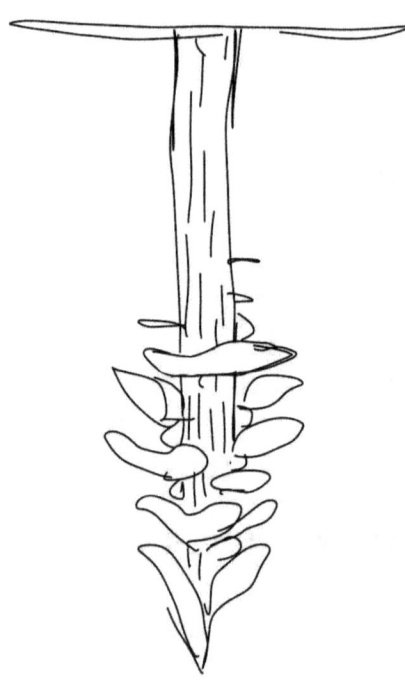

Woah...
   Oh my god,
   THAT'S ME.

   I can finally see
   This beautiful me,
   FINALLY FREE.

It's always been there,
You just weren't seeing it clear.

I saw your reflection at last,
And now it's in the past.

EVERYBODY CAN TELL YOU...

How beautiful you are,
How incredible you are.

BUT IT'S YOU...

    Who has to be it.

IT'S YOU WHO HAS TO FEEL IT...

        Know it,

            Embody it.

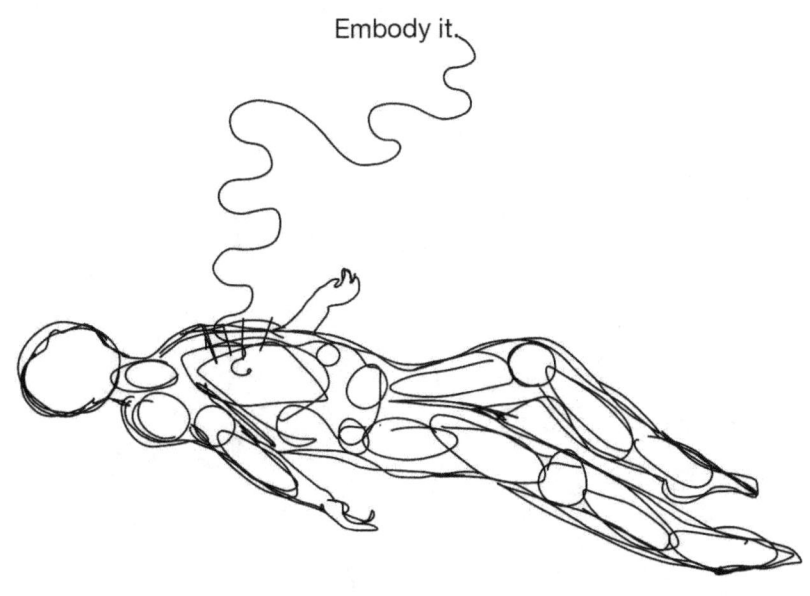

This life went so fast
IT COULDN'T LAST.

At last; it's in the past,
This ugly looking glass.

Take out the trash
Don't make it last.

**THROUGH THE LOOKING GLASS
NOTHING BUT THE PAST.**

Blast

       Blast,

              Pshhhhh....

                    'BLAST OFF!'

Cast off
Set your sail
Now, you can feel.

**This is real; this is me,
LIVING IN REALITY.**

On your way
It's a new day.

Freedom slung
No more need to run.

Exploring new frays
On this new day,

        Goodbye all gray
        I AM HERE TO STAY.

                I AM HERE TO STAY

                    *I AM **HERE TO STAY.***

              I AM HERE TO STAY

          I AM HERE TO STAY.

     I AM HERE TO STAY

I AM HERE TO STAY.

   I AM HERE TO STAY

      I AM HERE TO STAY

NOW, IT'S IN THE PAST,
My reflection, at last.

AT LAST!

YOU SAW YOUR REFLECTION AT LAST,
And now it's in the past.

Woah...
    Look at how beautiful I am,
    Look at how incredible I am.

        Woah!
        OH, WOW...

        [chuckling, laughing]
        hm hm, heh heh, ha ha.

        Grinning from cheek to cheek,
        Knowing there's nothing left to seek.

        No words left to speak
        At the highest peak,
        Ending this depressing streak
        That made you weak.

        Speechless...
        Confounded by nature,
        Surrounded by beauty.

        Stillness envelops your soul,
        Making you whole, once again.

To my biggest bully,

I FORGIVE YOU...
I forgive you FOR YOUR AGGRESSION.

I FORGIVE YOU...
I forgive you FOR YOUR OBSESSION.

I FORGIVE YOU...
I forgive you FOR YOUR REPRESSION.

I forgive you for all the anger and fear,
That made danger so hard to see clear.

I forgive you for your reliance on violence,
An alliance with the opposite of kindness.

I forgive you for your blindness to presence,
Causing an absence of purity, resulting in insecurity.

I forgive you for your acting out with bouts of rage,
Taking center stage, at such a young age.

This page has turned, our struggle scorned...

Behind us, there's no looking back,
Discovering our true reflection, we once did lack.

For all the pain, all the suffering it caused, there's no remorse
As emotions coarse, part of an overarching force...

That spirit residing in each one of us.

Because of you, I am stronger;
No longer weak, I can truly speak.

I am fierce, not allowing words to pierce...

This shield, I've come to wield,
Released from suffering I once held.

For now, I am healed...

                    And, I forgive you.

*Be the change you want to be,
Don't settle for mediocrity.*

***I SAW MY REFLECTION AT LAST,
AND NOW IT'S IN THE PAST.***

YOU ARE BEAUTIFUL.	I AM BEAUTIFUL.
YOU ARE KIND.	I AM KIND.
YOU ARE PEACEFUL.	I AM PEACFUL.
YOU ARE UNIQUE.	I AM NOT A FREAK.
YOU HAVE A LOT TO GIVE, WHEN YOU ALLOW YOURSELF TO FORGIVE.	I AM ABLE TO FORGIVE.
LOOK AT HOW INCREDIBLE YOU ARE.	I AM INCREDIBLE.

***YOU SAW YOUR REFLECTION AT LAST,
AND NOW IT'S IN THE PAST.***

I AM FINALLY FREE…

***TO BE, TO SEE,
ONLY THAT WHICH MAKES ME
HAPPY.***

ABOUT THE AUTHOR

*All my life I was hidden, my truth forbidden.
Stuck in the past, wondering how long it would all last.
Fast-forward to today, and I can finally say, "I've put my past away."*

*Hi, I'm Neal. When people ask me, "Where are you from?" I tell them,
"A universal home; is more real to me, than anything else."
Growing up, it wasn't always this way.*

*Watching a movie only wishing it to be true. Life was robotic.
Same patterns each day; observing others living out their dreams,
thinking something is not what it seems.*

*Alone, inside my head; no way to shed, an image everyone fed.
Where was I from? What had life become? Why wasn't it fun?
How will this illusion be undone?*

*Truth. By speaking truth to power.
I will no longer cower or feel sour because I've blossomed into a flower.*

*Where I'm from doesn't matter;
Nor, where I am going;
For, right here, right now,
This is home as I like to call it.*
-Neal The Earthling-

ARE YOU STRUGGLING WITH YOUR MENTAL HEALTH?

To often, people don't get the help they need when it comes to mental health struggles for a plethora of reasons.
Often not knowing where to even start.

If you can, talk to your primary care doctor or another health professional and ask them to connect you with the right mental health services.

If not and you or someone you know is suicidal or in emotional distress, contact the **National Suicide Prevention Lifeline.**
1-800-273-TALK (8255)

Or, to get general information on mental health and locate treatment services in your area contact SAMSHA,
the **Substance Abuse and Mental Health Service Administration.**
1-800-662-HELP (4357)

www.ingramcontent.com/pod-product-compliance
Lightning Source LLC
Chambersburg PA
CBHW071910070526
44583CB00016B/1927